Back Door
People

ALSO BY LEE PITTS

It's The Pitts
It's The Pitts Two
A Gentleman And A Scholar
The I Hate Chicken Cookbook
Tofu Free by '93
People Who Live At The End Of Dirt Roads

Back Door People

by
LEE PITTS

Illustrated by VEL MILLER

First Edition

Inquiries regarding this book should be addressed to:
Lee Pitts
P.O. Box 616
Morro Bay, CA 93443

Typeset by Charles R. Stocks, Inc.
Cover art and illustrations by Vel Miller
Printed by Image Graphics, Paducah, KY

ISBN No. 0-9666334-0-7

CONTENTS

Familiar Things 9

What Would You Have Done? 12

Born In A Barn 15

Splish Splash 18

The Father Of Our Country
  Was A Mother 21

Tradin' Places 24

I Do...Maybe 27

The Magic Of Babies 30

Field Guide 33

A Parent's Gift 36

In Or Out? 39

Back Door People 42

Hunk Of Burnin' Love 45

Read All About It 48

I'm Hung Up Right Now 51

Have You Got The Time? 54

Hat Check 57

CONTENTS

Give Us This Day. 60

My Passengers 63

Stuff I Don't Need. 66

Sacred Cows. 69

Ho Ho Hobo 72

Neighborin'. 75

Never Sleep Naked 78

Lost In America 81

The Flag Is Up. 84

Fair Time Is Fun Time 87

The Pedigree Of Man 90

Mechanical Bull. 93

When We Grow Up 96

Good Night. 99

Is Anybody There? 102

Cashing In The Chips 105

First, Last And Always 108

Country folks use the back door.
Out beyond the city limits anyone who comes to the front
door is usually selling something you don't need or want.
Back door people are more trusting.
These are the same people who don't lock their cars.
They would have no idea where to find a house key.
Wise mothers insist their kids use the rear entrance,
and when they grow up they'll be better adults as a result.
Thanks Mom, for making me a back door person.
This book is dedicated to you.

FAMILIAR THINGS

We all keep them around... old, worn out things past their prime. No, we are not talking spouses, simply stuff. The objects that clutter our lives that we spend a lifetime collecting. The rubble of our existence. A favorite flannel shirt that would not make a decent rag or a lucky pair of socks with holes where the toes should be. Even the poorest person has them, worthless but familiar things that we value more than gold.

We retain them for the memories and the security they provide. A father keeps an old pair of jeans that never fit in the first place because the grass stain on the knee reminds him of a game on the grass with the kids. A mother saves boxes of baby clothes long after the last child has left home because old clothes are the fabric of our lives. Those old slippers with worn down soles may torture the feet but they still provide comfort for the soul.

It is why we must keep a constant vigil on the trash can. You never know when someone might mistake for litter an old ball glove, a tattered blanket or a faded photograph. If these treasures were to vanish in a garage sale it would be like losing a little part of yourself. You can call it being old fashioned, or just wanting a bit of our old world back, but there is more to it than that. After spending a lifetime saying good-bye to dear relatives and old friends we all need something ageless and everlasting to hang on to. How else do you explain our fondness for classic cars, old trees and antique glassware?

Not that we shouldn't redo, remodel, refurbish, revamp or refresh on occasion. We need to rearrange the furniture in our lives once in a while, but that does not mean we should get rid of father's chair with the familiar lumps in all the right places just because it's a little faded and frayed. So too is father. We admire the latest fashion or the newest hairdo just as long as it's worn by the same wonderful woman.

Change is good, we all must grow. But in a world that is moving at kilobytes per second we also need an anchor to tie to once in a while. That explains why we reelect shady politicians. We are more comfortable with familiar crooks than unacquainted ones. Rather than experience the fear of the unknown we go back to the same dentist with big rough hands, the banker who never smiles and the grocery checker who always does, because we know what to expect from these folks.

We need familiar guideposts if we are to find our way in life. A cottonwood tree, a crumbling barn or a church steeple not only decorate our world, they serve as signposts on our journey. If they were to disappear we would feel the same loss we experience when we see a moving van pull up next door or a favorite store going out of business.

It's not that we aren't adventurous. We will sample the roasted rattlesnake on the menu and partake of exotic locales but they'll never replace hamburgers and home as the staples of our lives. We'll try the "new and improved version" but sometimes we just want old and reliable, tried and true, Betty Crocker® and Aunt Jemima®.

We are no different than the animal that comes back to her birthplace to have a baby or the trucker who stops at the same truck stop on the interstate every trip. We are just looking for a little consistency in our lives. Without it we are lost like the child without a father or the homeless without a home.

We receive warmth from the fact that the sun will come up in the same place tomorrow. We are reassured by the regularity of the tides, made peaceful by the enduring majesty of a mountain and grounded in the soil of the earth. We are nurtured by familiar friends, take solace in recurring miracles and made secure in the comfort of an old shoe.

WHAT WOULD YOU HAVE DONE?

God couldn't be everywhere so he made babysitters. One of God's grandest creations was a cow we called "Mom." Mom was our babysitting cow, and was she something special.

Mom invariably had four or five calves with her in addition to her own. Other cows, on their way to get a drink at the local watering trough, would drop their calves off with her and they were never in any hurry to retrieve them. I don't know if the other cows ever thanked Mom or brought her flowers for babysitting their spoiled kids.

Mom was one of those special cows who just seemed to like the patter of little hooves around her. When she treated herself to a drink of water she did so with a dozen calves frolicking about.

She surrendered every pleasure and sacrificed every comfort. At feeding time Mom didn't run to the hay truck like the other moms, but stayed patiently behind babysitting the neighborhood bed wetters.

She would eat the hay if you took it to her general vicinity but she always shared it with her extended family. She didn't butt the calves away either, like the other moms did, when they stood in the middle of the hay and went tinkle. Mom's was truly an unselfish love.

I think the calves often took Mom for granted too. When they got thirsty, and their own mothers were nowhere to be seen, they butted the bag of their adopted mother. I guess Mom figured if she had to carry it around between her legs she might as well use it. There were a lot of things that Mom needed worse than extra mouths to feed. She was as thin as a rail. But if Mom had any milk she'd freely give it.

All this is not to suggest that Mom shirked her responsibilities in caring for her own calf. As you would expect, she was a devoted mother. Mom and her own calf seemed to never part company and when they arrived at the weaning pen the skinny Mom seemed to look with motherly pride upon her calf. Which, by the way, was always the biggest.

After three days of bellering the other cows forgot about their calves and no longer hung around the weaning pen. But Mom stayed around for ten days after the trucks had departed, crying for her own calf and no doubt several others.

As usual, we were not prepared when tragedy struck. I guess I had just assumed that an animal with such motherly instincts would automatically get bred every year. The veterinarian could not have seen my heart sink as he withdrew his arm and pronounced our favorite cow… "Open." In her old age she had given so much of herself and got so run down that she failed to breed back.

The vet painted a big zero on her rump and I cut her switch, an indication of her "openness." This is how I showed my gratitude? This is the thanks Mom got for being a good mother?

An argument raged within me. Everyone knows a good cattle-man doesn't keep open cows around. They provide no income and it would cost more than a couple hundred dollars to keep her for another year. I tried to convince myself that there would be a special place in heaven for the babysitting cow we called Mom.

I left her in the corral awaiting a ride to her final destination. But the next day when I went to load her up to take her to the auction Mom wasn't in the pen. It seems that some sentimental old fool had accidentally left the corral gate open.

BORN IN A BARN

IN A CLASSY RESTAURANT a little boy burped so loud I wondered where the epicenter was. My first reaction was to dive under a table. The boy's belch must have registered a 5.5 on the Richter Scale! Whatever happened to the idea that children were "to be seen and not heard"? The father's reaction to his child, and I use both familial terms in the loosest sense, was one of great pride. While the mother, in a voice that would remove wallpaper, painted the air with cuss words about her son's bad manners.

I was shocked by the young boy's behavior. But then I am a relic from an era when your manners reflected on your parents and you were constantly reminded to remember whose boy you were. Sure, kids have always thought it cool to be offensive but previous generations eventually outgrew this childish behavior.

Manners are just one more thing kids aren't learning in school these days. I'm not referring to Emily Post, which fork to use or how to hold your pinkie in the air while sipping tea. I'm talking simple, common decency here! For example, as I write this I am attempting to concentrate while listening to the ultimate in rudeness … a leaf blower. My neighbor is blowing his dust on to my property at deafening decibels and later he will bring his dog over to use my lawn.

This epidemic of bad manners is all around us. The air is filled with bad perfume, "good" cigars and loud music from boom boxes so large they must be transported in the back of trucks. Telemarketers call during supper, fast food diners crowd in line and skateboarding scamps run you off the sidewalk. Athletic role models spit like ballplayers and scratch like their clothes were full of fleas. People "pick" their teeth in public and I'm not talking about selecting new dentures. Go downtown and you'll see people so dirty they need to wash BEFORE they use the restroom. And driving these days? Forget it. Bad manners are the leading cause of death on our nation's highways. You can get shot just for looking at someone!

Cussing has become so common our ears have dulled to the sound. Profanity has perpetrated our movies, our music and our culture. I can remember when obscenities were not used in front of women but now even their conversations are laced with four letter words. Men use words with sexual overtones to impress the ladies with their sexual prowess. Although they may talk a good game, I really doubt that profanity is one of the things a classy lady is looking for in a man.

Speaking of women, the last time anyone held a door open for a female was the door of a pay toilet so someone could be cheated out of a dime. I understand that women want to be treated equally so why not hold the door open for everyone? Man or woman, black or white.

It is said that the difference between man and animal is that man is rational. Anyone who pays any attention to politics would quickly realize this is simply not true. The real difference between man and beast is that people can be polite. We live by unwritten rules of decency and proper behavior that decree donkeys don't drive and men have manners. Cows can't say *please, thank you, excuse me* and *you're welcome,* but people should. The difference between pigs and people is that it's acceptable for swine to chew with their mouths open. Creatures scratch and sniff wherever and whenever they want but they are animals. Hogs run over their siblings to be the first in line at the milk bar but they were born in a barn. What's your excuse?

Manners do matter. If we fail to adhere to rules of decorum we face further breakdown of our civilized society. It's no coincidence that the word "civilization" has at its root the word "civil." As in, being civil to one another. Get it?

SPLISH SPLASH

My wife and I have a mixed marriage, she takes baths whereas I prefer a refreshing shower. There really are only two kinds of people in this world, those who splish in the shower and those who splash in the tub. All right, okay, I know what you are thinking. There is a third category and I must admit these "deodorant deprived persons of scent" are easy to spot, or should I say smell? I think we all know people who turn on the faucet in the wash basin, dabble a few drops on their face to get the sleep out of their eyes and consider themselves clean.

For the rest of us the question is, do we scour sitting or standing? Personally, I have detested baths ever since as the middle child I was forced to bathe in tepid second-hand suds left behind by my older brother. I didn't know what "being in hot water" meant until I got married. I contend that is the reason why my brother grew up clean, well dressed and respectable and why I adorn myself in hand-me-downs and dread Saturday nights.

The last bath I took was with a bunch of five year olds in the shallow end of the community swimming pool twenty years ago. Needless to say, I came out feeling dirtier than when I went in. Oh, that's not quite right. I have taken a couple baths lately. A financial one in the cattle business and the sponge bath a nurse gave me in the hospital. I must say I preferred the bovine variety.

I'll probably find myself in hot water for saying so but baths are basically a sex thing. Men take showers whereas women, celebrities and investment bankers take bubble baths. The problem with working men taking baths is they leave behind an oil slick worse than the Exxon Valdez. And I've seen some men who, if they sat down in a tub, would displace all the water. Let's face it, baths are disgusting. Who wants to sit in your own muddy water? Soak in your own soil? Frolic in your own filth?

Not me.

Baths are for lazy people who want to lay down on the job and let the dirt just soak off. But if you've ever emptied a dipping vat and seen what was left behind by the creatures that were dipped, you'd realize just how disgusting baths are. It is impossible to take a bath without getting something else dirty.

There are several advantages to showering. It is quicker and there is less chance of drowning. There is no ring around the tub left to clean and every part of your body gets wet. The only anatomical components that do not come clean are the bottoms of your feet, but who's looking at them?

Relax in the bath tub and what is the first thing that happens?

That's right, the telephone rings. Take a shower and you can't hear the phone ring above your singing. In the shower you can't sit on the soap either. Ouch, does that hurt?

Some people compromise and install "jets" in their tub. But a whirlpool is nothing more than a horizontal shower. I have heard that in some cultures they take a bath first and then rinse with a shower. But that seems like too much work for something you'll have to repeat in a week anyway.

In western movies, cowboys and sodbusters are always pictured smoking a big cigar while buried in a five cent bubble bath. This is supposed to be their reward after working in the fields or at the conclusion of a long trail drive. But this is revisionist history. The real reason Hollywood directors cover farmer's and rancher's bodies in suds in a tub is so that the viewer won't be exposed to their gnarled, pale and X-rated bodies. Put that same cowboy or farmer in the shower and it would be the scariest shower scene since Psycho.

THE FATHER OF OUR COUNTRY WAS A MOTHER

IT IS THE DUMBEST QUESTION I've ever heard, without a doubt. "What do you want, a boy or a girl?" I cringe when I hear an expectant couple being asked that question.

It's as if parents today are selecting a pet dog or a flavor of ice cream cone. Of course, most people answer that stupid question in one of two ways; either they want a boy or they want their next child to be a grandchild.

Nine out of ten first time parents when asked what their sexual preference is will answer, "We are hoping for a boy." Only after having one will they then wish for a baby girl. Parents want a boy so he can grow up to be President, play in the big leagues or follow in father's footsteps, even if he has to jump bail to do so.

Today, when an expectant couple finds out, even before the child is born, that it will be a girl their thoughts immediately turn from presidential aspirations to selecting the silver pattern for her Barbie Doll®. We want girl babies to love, nurture and dress in frilly clothes.

We want boys so they can grow up to be the strongest or the richest man in the world.

This emphasis on maleness seems ridiculous to me because if it weren't for females all of us males would still be running around in dirty diapers. It was our moms who took time out of their busy lives to introduce us to life's finer things, such as the toilet. Oh sure, your father was probably out working, bringing home the bacon, but it was your mother who played life's most demanding role. It was she who tucked you in at night, always preached to you about wearing clean underwear and taught you not to blow bubbles in your milk. It was your mother who cleaned the pony tracks off the living room carpet and made you eat chicken soup when you were sick.

As I recall, I never had a man teacher until I was in the ninth grade and by then it didn't matter because the women in my life had already taught me everything I needed to know. The poorly paid women taught me when I was stupid. And they taught me the important things in life such as never lose your lunch money, but it's okay to share it. It was a woman who taught me to read, count and what was proper to show and tell. Those lady teachers were stepmother and babysitter to several generations when teaching was considered women's work. Oh sure, the principal was a man, he got paid more but he didn't do any of the dirty work. If a man had taught me to count I would probably think that after nine and ten came jack, queen and king. Man may educate the world but woman has always educated man!

Men may run most of the banks of this world but it is the women who do the really important work like being den mothers and PTA volunteers. When drunken maniacs, mostly men, were slaughtering people on our nation's highways it was Mothers Against Drunk Driving who made us MADD enough to start doing something about it.

If we'd have been raised by our fathers we'd all be dirty, illiterate smart alecks living on spaghetti sandwiches and cream filled cookies. Our fathers were probably elated when the doctor first informed him, "It's a Boy!" But now that you are forty and are a baseball card collector instead of a major league third baseman and a bookie instead of an investment banker your dad is probably a little disappointed. But your mother, well, she's still waiting patiently for some sign of improvement.

TRADIN' PLACES

THEY LEFT THE AUCTION shrouding their eyes, not caring to stand by and watch the sale of their cows. The ones they had raised from calves and given family names. We make "failure" such a public spectacle and they wanted no one to see their tears.

They'd best be getting on with their lives. The married couple wasn't getting any younger and the bank wanted its money. So, they sold the old ranch house and moved their possessions to town in the back of their gooseneck trailer. When it was empty the truck was traded in on something a bit more practical. The ranch pickup wouldn't fit in the garage of the tract home anyway. A few items were left behind, kind of as a house warming present for the new owners, but they were soon stacked by the road, "free for hauling away." Only one item was broken in the move to town, an antique vase, like the ranch, handed down from generation to generation.

Having lived their entire lives under cowboy hats they didn't have the necessary skills or the proper clothes for urban life. Too many buckles and boots. Having said good-bye to their horses and their habits they tried to rid their lives of any record of the ranch. It was bad enough when a cattle truck would pass or a cowboy friend would call. They didn't need mementos or trinkets reminding them of better days.

City life took some getting used to. You couldn't run through the house half dressed because a salesman might be standing at the door. They had never locked their door in the country and were not accustomed to carrying a house key. So now they had to leave a window cracked so they could crawl back in the house. The neighbors complained about their barking dog, but not for long. Never having been one to stay cooped up in a corral, he got bored to death. Run over by a car.

Admittedly, town life had some pluses. If you were baking and ran out of milk a store or a neighbor was handy. And when you flushed your toilet it was someone else's problem. There was no well to go dry and fast food was readily available.

He had never gone to college, having always known what he would do for a living. Finally, he got a job delivering soda pop which meant he had to change the brand he drank. In his spare time he wandered around like a pony with its bridle off. One day he drove out beyond the urban sprawl, past the ranchettes to the old home place. They had traded places with an urban-bred family looking for "the simple life." Oh, really? Wait till the septic tank backed up or the road went out. Now they were living in each other's world. Maybe it would be different for them. Perhaps they'd make it. After all, there wasn't a cow on the place; just a llama, a non-working breed of dog and a miniature horse. They had probably never swung their leg over the back of a real horse anyway. No sagebrush rebels these.

The old home had metamorphosed into a bed and breakfast with a coat of paint and a sign by the road. The tree house was taken down for insurance purposes, no doubt. A cute riding mower became the first tractor to take up permanent residence on the place in three generations. The new garden sprouted signs the newcomers knew as much about farming as a hog does about Sundays. It was planted too early in the spring and there were far too many mounds of zucchini.

So this is the changing landscape of the countryside; "where everyone has a gardener or is one." Welcome to a world that is moving at Internet speed and doesn't seem to care too much for the "family" or the "farm." Where heritage, traditions and customs are reduced to being part of an irrelevant past.

But the blood, sweat and tears won't sift from the soil that easily.

I DO ... MAYBE

My FRIEND, CHARLIE SPECK, (we call him Fly Speck) is getting married next month and he is already anticipating marital problems. This is understandable since the last time he went through a "change of wife" she cleaned him out down to his long handled underwear. It was a messy divorce with lawyers, private detectives and accountants. They ended up having a custody battle over the twelve year old stereo.

Not wanting to repeat such an ugly experience, Fly naturally came to me to help him draw up one of those prenuptial agreements that all the rich people in Hollywood sign. Knowing that there may be others that could quite possibly have the same need, I drew up sort of a Cowboy Prenuptial. I'm happy to share it with you now with fervent hopes it might save some people from having to deal with unsavory folks like former spouses and attorneys. Here goes ...

"Wherefore marriage is the chief cause of divorce and seeing as how divorce is the primary cause of poverty, and seeing as how Fly and Sally Mae already have five marriages between them; therefore, be it hereby known by everybody that in the event of a divorce between Fly and Sally Mae their assets shall be divided as follows:

Sally can keep all the jewelry given to her by Fly during their courtship including the mood ring, horseshoe belt buckle and glow in the dark earrings that also double as fishing lures. She can also keep the cubic zirconium wedding ring but must be responsible for the payments on the ring down at the finance company.

Fly shall keep all family heirlooms passed down to him from his long lost relatives including the silver plated snuff can lid, hand carved pool cue made from the reproductive organ of a bull, authentic stuffed road kill armadillo and his extensive seed cap collection.

In the event that there shall be any money saved during the marriage Sally shall get custody of it but she must return the coin wrappers it came in. The matching luggage shall be divided equally with Fly taking the plastic grocery luggage bags and Sally taking possession of the paper luggage sacks.

Because Fly is a working cowboy he shall keep his horse, saddle and tack but Sally can have the shotgun if she pays the interest due at the pawn shop, and promises not to use it on her husband. Fly shall be forced to take the dog in lieu of alimony payments.

In the event there will be any children as a result of this union they shall be the sole possession of Sally Mae. Fly will get the kids for brandings and hay season but never during any holidays or hunting season when it may be an inconvenience. "Child support" from Fly shall consist of patting the kids on the back and saying, "well done," at the appropriate times.

Sally can keep the couple's home but she must remove it from the pickup. This is only fair because the camper shell was a wedding present from her father. The truck shall be the property of Fly, including the gun rack and curtains from a previous marriage.

Fly does reserve the right to leave at any minute including the middle of the night. Both parties to this marriage do hereby agree not to hire any lawyers, marriage counselors or paid assassins."

THE MAGIC OF BABIES

WHAT IS IT ABOUT BABIES? They pout and poop and we ooh and aah. They go goo goo and we go gaa gaa. It is truly one of life's great mysteries. They cost a fortune, attract in-laws like a magnet, cry constantly, spit up and smell funny and yet we love them more than life itself.

What is this magic these angels from heaven possess?

It has been suggested that we love babies so much because they are helpless creatures who cannot carry on an intelligent discussion and are totally dependent on others for their livelihood. But if that were the case politicians would be more well liked. I have heard that bald babies are the most "lovable" but I have even less hair now than I did as an infant and I have yet to meet a woman with the urge to pick me up and smother me with hugs and kisses like they would a hairless infant.

Newly arrived farm animals possess this bewitching magic too. The season of birth has always been my favorite time of the year on the ranch. There is nothing quite like waking every two hours to check on amateur heifers or expectant ewes, although I do wish my wife would be more considerate of others when she does so. If something goes wrong these babies become permanent members of our household. When darkness falls it's not uncommon to have calves in the bathtub, bunnies in the oven, puppies on the porch and veterinarians over for dinner.

The magic of babies is as mystifying to me as the commitment of motherhood. Cattle are not usually thought of as inspiring brutes but one has to marvel at a creature that will strain for hours in freezing weather, enduring hours of pain in order to pop out an oversized, slimy hair ball through an opening the size of a grapefruit. Then she will lick the baby lovingly and guard it with her life. Why doesn't she just take off running when she has the chance like a deadbeat dad would do? It is said sheep are stupid but the only mother I've ever seen abandon her babies was a ewe who took one look at her quadruplets, realized she was not up to the task, and immediately vacated the county.

No animal stays cute forever. There is nothing prettier than a piglet and nothing quite as ugly as an old sow. We all love kittens before they open their eyes but wait eight weeks and no one can envision them as permanent pets. If a day-old chick poops in your hand you laugh and say, "How precious!" Ten weeks later you have no compunction about eating that chicken in the form of a drumstick.

When do infants lose their magic? What changes in their personality that makes them mundane? For rabbits it's when they begin to reproduce and cats when they start to shed. Children lose much of their allure long before they start to drive and date, about the time they start to talk and eat solid food. You may cry when your child leaves home but it probably has more to do with losing a tax deduction than the fact that they could still make your heart melt with a smile.

I wish I knew what makes babies so adorable, we could all use a shot of it. Maybe it's because infants are such simple creatures. They really don't ask for much: a hug when they're lonely, a blanket when they're cold, food when they're famished, a nap when they're tired and clean pants every so often. That's not too much to ask, is it? We should all be satisfied with as much.

If I had to guess, I'd say we love babies so dearly because of the promise they hold for the future. A cattleman sees a calf as an advancement in animal husbandry. A horseman hopes for a winner with every foal and a proud parent looks at a toddler and envisions a President, an All Star or an anesthesiologist. In babies we see renewal, not a second chance at life, but of renewed hope for the species. An improvement in the bloodline.

FIELD GUIDE

FOR GOLFERS WHO really missed the fairway and hunters who don't know the difference between a moose and an animal that goes "moo," I have composed a pocket guide to farm animals. This handbook should make it easier for dudes from the city to identify common farm animals and make their journey more rewarding next time they venture into the great outdoors.

Sheep - That large dog-sized animal you see in flocks all over the west in plentiful supply, well, those are NOT sheep. Those are coyotes or government relocated wolves. Catching a glimpse of a real sheep in the countryside is becoming an extremely rare occurrence. If you think you see one you should attempt to document your vision with a photograph.

Dentition is often used for positive identification of sheep, the lamb being the deceased animal with teeth marks around its neck. Sheep have become extremely rare due to two primary natural predators: coyotes and imports. Sheep are poor swimmers, natural followers, blend well into the landscape and spend most of their time looking for ways to die in new and creative ways.

Cow - This is the most recognizable animal to motorists passing by on the interstate. Most people refer to every animal they see as a cow, including bulls, llamas and horses. When a bored child spending vacation in the back seat of the family car asks a parent what animal or plant they are presently passing the answer is always, "cows" or "corn." Even if it's buffalo or broccoli.

What makes a cow, a cow, is the fact that it has given birth to a calf, an irregular occurrence that has been chiefly responsible for the economic ruin of the common cowboy (see below). Despite what you may have heard, cows do not bite, sting or cause global warming. They are pacifists by nature. If you observe one snorting, stamping its feet and bellering it's merely the cow's way of welcoming you to the countryside. The primary enemies of cows are vegetarians, short sighted hunters, Mad Cow Disease, fast cars and slow truckers. Cows are found in extremely dry climates where it never rains. They CAN'T be found in New York City or Washington DC, although politicians in those places have been known to leave behind the same by-product.

Horse - There are two species of horses. The habitat of the functional strain is private property; whereas, the breeding ground for the second type of horse is federally owned land. The government variety is wild, eats expensive food and isn't good for anything but reproducing more of the same. But enough about bureaucrats.

Privately owned horses are usually well mannered and gainfully employed.

In distinguishing horses from other animals such as cows, sheep and cowboys, remember that horses always smell better when sweaty, look more desirable in leather and their meat is considered inedible, except in France.

Cowboy - A hairy mammal that is identified by the presence of skin cancer, missing digits, bowed legs, arthritic joints and an ever present baseball cap. Anyone wearing a cowboy hat is probably a truck driver or country western singer. The cowboy leaves behind the easily distinguished footprint of a boot.

The natural habitat of this creature is open range where the sky is not cloudy all day. Cowboys don't do well raised in captivity and can be found wherever there are cows and cowgirls. All cowboys undertake an annual migration in search of a new job. The sexes are usually kept separate except during breeding season and the common cowboy assumes no responsibility in caring for its young. They are active feeders both night and day. If backed into a corner most cowboys should be considered extremely dangerous. DO NOT irritate the beast.

A PARENT'S GIFT

THE "AMERICAN DREAM" is no longer owning a home. It is getting the offspring to move out of that home. Or, so say some parents. But when the day actually arrives for the brood to leave the nest Mom can think of all kinds of excuses why the child should remain in adult day-care forever. When kids go off to college or to make a date with the world, parents worry they may not return. Even if they do come back to visit every parent knows the child shall be forever changed by that first flight. When sons and daughters come home for the holidays they'll no longer sit at the kid's table. They may even join in a toast and drink alcohol for the first time in front of their folks. This is NOT cause for celebration.

Parents who let their youngsters hunt with guns and ride pitching ponies are all of a sudden concerned about the dangers of college math. Heaven forbid their child should be exposed to an x-rated movie or an adult nightclub. When a ranch kid goes off to college Mom and Dad invariably become distressed about their driving;

although, they never worried when a child, whose feet didn't reach the peddles, drove the feed truck.

Parents worry that when their child is turned loose on the world without adult supervision he or she will grow their hair in purple spikes, go vegetarian and become a nose-ringed poet. This despite never having displayed a talent for rhyming words or liking squash. There is grave concern your baby will soon make you a grandparent because they don't know how babies are made; although, they have been around lambing ewes, lusty bulls and MTV since they wore long pants. Even though you were married at 17 years of age your kids should wait until middle age to marry. Child bearing should be put off until the grandparents want more grandchildren.

Sister and brother can field dress a deer but Mom worries they may go hungry at college. The poor child was raised on fast food and cream filled cupcakes but Dad hopes they'll "eat right" away from home. Parents who force fed their kids a three course meal consisting of a peanut butter and jelly sandwich, corn chips and a soda, now send junior off to college with a set of pots and pans, a cookbook and recipe cards.

Here's a child who hasn't made a bed or hung up clothes since first grade and all of a sudden mom and pop are concerned about their flossing habits. Or credit card balances. "Money isn't everything," you taught your kids wisely, only to realize that for the next four years it very well could be.

You can't fool me. Parents are sad when their kids leave home because the nest will be empty and the humor, companionship and free labor will be gone. Father may actually have to mow the lawn and mom will inherit even more chores than usual. Their job as parents is about to be graded by a tough teacher: the real world.

Relax mom and dad. The world is ready for your child. A kid raised amongst rattlesnakes, lightning strikes and charging bulls ought to be able to handle coed dorms. You've done your job. Hopefully, you've given your child a good pedigree and reason to live up to it. Just don't expect thank yous or letters, except ones requesting more money.

Look at the bright side, for the first time when your telephone rings, it may actually be for you. And the grocery bill and laundry pile will go down, except twice a year when the wayward child comes home bearing big bulging bags.

Tomorrow has turned into today and the time has come to let go. Be gentle kind world. You have reluctantly been given a parent's greatest gift.

IN OR OUT?

THERE REALLY ARE only two kinds of people in this world. Those who let their pets in the house and those who don't. I happen to be a member of the more intelligent class of people who believe if God had meant for dogs to enter the residence he would NOT have given them skin diseases that make them scratch their privates in public.

Of course I am referring to real dogs such as Border Collies, Kelpies, Shepherds, Labs and Rotts, not those cute little toy dogs that serve as one bite appetizers to real dogs. Those tiny little things with pink bows that need their hair styled aren't really dogs. They'd probably die or end up as frozen dog-sicles if exposed to the elements, so it's probably all right that you let them sleep in the thermostatically controlled house.

Show me a home where a dog lives and I'll show you a dirty house, unless of course you have the dog's hair shampooed and trimmed once a week at a salon. If that's the case it may be cheaper just to buy your dog his own humble abode.

The inside dog simply creates far too many problems. It's hard enough getting the man of the house to wipe the mud and manure off his feet before walking on your white shag carpet. How are you going to convince a dog to wipe his?

This business of getting up at three in the morning to let the dog outside for his constitutional, whose idea was that? If the dog was outside to begin with you wouldn't need to wake it up to let it out, now, would you? And if you accidentally oversleep what happens? The dog has an "accident." At least that's what they call it. I think they do it on purpose.

I read a story somewhere about a dog that had actually been taught to use the toilet. That's great, but can you imagine? Now in addition to your teenagers urging you to, "speed things up in there," your dog is scratching on the door to use the facilities as well. No thank you very much. On second thought, you could blame the dog for leaving the seat up!

Let a dog in the house for just five minutes and he thinks it's his paw print on the deed. A house dog always takes over the best chair in the house, if he hasn't already chewed the legs off. And they are constantly under foot. At dinner time the house dog can usually be found begging for scraps at the dinner table. This can be convenient for getting rid of distasteful food but it can ruin your appetite and run up big bills at the veterinary clinic.

House dogs demand your complete attention. Relax for a moment and the mutt is in your face expecting you to rub him in that spot that makes his leg jerk uncontrollably. Or, for you to throw a toy for him to retrieve. Don't they ever tire of this game?

Then there are the social aspects of having a dog in the house. You can't have a good argument with your wife because she refuses to argue in front of the dog. And when company comes to your house your average ranch dog sniffs them all over before burying his head in embarrassing parts of their anatomy.

As bad as house dogs are, cats are even worse. The only reason to have a cat in the house is so the dog will have something to munch on while it's watching television.

Oh, I suppose there are some advantages to having a dog in the house. They are cleaner than teenagers and better conversationalists than most husbands. You'll always have an excuse when a sock disappears out of the dryer or three dozen cookies for your daughter's classroom come up missing. You can always blame the dog for the ring around the tub, the mysterious pungent odor and …

"Whose hair is that on the collar of your shirt?"

BACK DOOR PEOPLE

Architects often design houses with fancy facades and decorative doors on the front. But like a sauna or bomb shelter they seldom get used. Country folks use the back door.

In the country anyone who comes to the front door is usually selling something you don't need or want. Even the dogs know the difference. Dogs don't bite back door people, they are more apt to lick them to death. But let a stranger approach the front door and those same dogs will show their teeth, growl and suggest they are not welcome. Dogs are very suspicious of front door people.

Back door people are more trusting. These are the same people who don't lock their cars. They would have no idea where to find a key for the house.

If a neighbor stops by with some vegetables they don't bother to knock. They just pop their head in the back door and yell, "Yoo-hoo, it's just me!" If no one is home they'll leave whatever they brought on the back porch to be discovered later when it starts to smell.

There may still be a working doorbell by the front door but if someone rang it those inside would probably answer the phone instead of the door.

Even the U.P.S. driver knows to come to the back door. If a substitute driver should happen to leave a fruit cake Christmas present by the front door it might not be discovered until Labor Day. (Who would know the difference?)

The country home is usually designed so that the back door connects to a back porch, or mud room, as it is sometimes known. It's called that because there is enough accumulated top soil there to grow a garden. In the summer the dirty boots sit by the boot scraper by the back door. In the winter they are taken off inside along with the dirty pants and rain slickers that have collected over three generations. There is a mat to wipe one's feet but nobody does; instead, the mat serves as a mattress for the dog.

If a family member is particularly dirty from plowing a dusty field or wrestling calves, the woman of the house usually yells from the kitchen, "Don't go tromping through the house with those filthy clothes on!" So the dirty clothes are left by the back door while the defrocked family member streaks through the house to the bathroom. No one would ever dream of taking off all their clothes by the front door and running through the dining room.

Really, the back door is usually two doors. In the winter the wife pleads, "Please close the back door so we don't catch our death from cold." And in the summer she yells, "Don't slam the screen door!"

That could never happen with the front door. It's been stuck shut for years.

The back door connects to the back porch which almost always connects to the kitchen. The heart of the house. The front door, on the other hand, connects to a darkened entry way that is seldom used. The wood panels on the front door have cracked and the paint is peeling. Birds have made a nest right above the front door, figuring it would be the most undisturbed part of the house. Spiders have spun their cobwebs across the front door and those flimsy strands might as well be protective iron bars. They keep the burglars out. The light bulb by the front door went out years ago.

I wonder … when does the back door become the front door?

HUNK OF BURNIN' LOVE

SOCIETY HAS MADE rapid progress in freeing people from back breaking work so they have more leisure time to go to the gym and do back breaking workouts. The modern fitness center has made it possible TO PAY instead of BEING PAID for sweating. At the gym you could recline in a tanning booth if you didn't have the time to get a real tan, because you were at the gym getting a fake one. Is this making sense to anyone?

Working out at a gym is not primarily about building better bodies anyway, you can pay a plastic surgeon to do that. It's about MEETING better bodies. The gym has become the singles bar for people who don't drink. Besides, by going to a gym you can meet a higher class of people, those whose body language and clothes seem to say, "I'm better than you because I don't do any physical work for a living."

I learned all this because my friend Roany got his spurs all tangled up and fell in love. That's right, Cupid shot him through the heart. But before he could go to courtin' properly Roany had to get his body in shape, "buffed up," as they say. Not that I've looked, mind you, but Roany seemed to have an acceptable body to me, for a cowboy. He had four limbs, nine fingers and some hair. It's just that Roany had always lived by the motto, "Live fast, die young and leave behind an ugly corpse."

Roany's not fat. If he closed one eye he'd look like a needle. He's strong too, from years of lifting bales, cutting the ranch owner's meat and bench pressing metal panels off his chest. But Roany told me he needed work on different muscle groups. Heaven knows Roany had body parts other than his "abs" that needed fixing a whole lot worse. His face is so ugly he could eat oats out of a churn and giving Roany bigger muscles would be like putting lipstick on a pig. But Roany needed moral support and so I tagged along with him to the fitness center.

Looking at my body I know it's hard to believe but I don't hang around gyms much. I found this one well equipped though, and the machinery was nice too. The smell of testosterone filled the air and the women weren't wearing enough clothes to dust a fiddle. I must admit their aerobics left me breathless and I had to exercise a great deal of restraint because some of those women were showing a little too much equipment, if you know what I mean? I got the feeling some people go to the gym just to wear the compulsory clothes, in that respect it's a lot like line dancing.

After my "minimal workout" I needed a cooling off period so I introduced myself to my personal trainer. Jim had muscles on top his muscles and was so large he could derail a freight train. I could just envision a leotard clad housewife telling her husband over sugar flakes, "I think I'll go to Jim today."

Exercise has entered the machine age. Yuppies gabbed breathlessly on cell phones as they walked on tread mills, climbed stair steppers, skied cross country and bicycled. All without going anywhere. There ought to be some way to harness this unproductive sweat. The machines were computerized to indicate how many calories were being "burned." Jim said, "A good work out has to burn, baby, burn."

I was totally burned out from my exercise in futility and needed a little post workout refreshment before my daily nap. So, I went to round up Roany. It turned out that Cupid's arrow hit Roany but missed his prospective girlfriend entirely. Either that or she was no longer interested in Roany after seeing him in a Speedo®. Alas, Roany had met resistance in his workout and I tried to console him. "Let's go down to the Dairy Queen® and burn a couple calories waiting in line for a triple fudge sundae," I said. "As long we stay away from this place and keep all our clothes on our bodies we don't have to look that good anyway."

READ ALL ABOUT IT

WE ARE SUFFERING from a bad news overload in this country and the latest casualties are big city newspapers. Many are in financial trouble. The black ink has turned to red. I learned this news in one of those daily papers that weighs more than your first baby at birth and makes about as much sense. "Filled with all the news that's fit to forget," should be their motto. But smaller weekly papers are doing fine, thank you very much.

It seems there's a limit to how much "news" we can take. For most of us a once a week dose is all we really need. Besides, the cities are making bad news faster than we can digest it. And their newspapers have lost their local flavor.

"If it bleeds it leads" doesn't go down well in towns where people have a good chance of dying of natural causes instead of drive-bys and drugs. We are more interested in reading about the community in which we live than the latest tragedy in a foreign country we collectively couldn't find on a map. It's not that we've grown cold or callous, it's just that if there is a local tragedy we can do something about it, like hand deliver a casserole, hold a benefit barbecue or a community car wash.

Small town newspapers are as unique as the towns they represent and so are their names: The Advance, Sounder, Nugget, Blade and Clarion. The Press Democrat and Republican Ledger may paper the same town but their names have nothing to do with their politics. They hold themselves to lofty goals and high standards these papers: The Leader, Enterprise, Neighbor and Citizen. While others don't take themselves quite so seriously: DeQueen Bee, The Rustler and The Tumbleweed.

The weekly newspaper is the community bulletin board with announcements of bingo games, church services, class reunions and 4-H meetings. The old joke is that in small towns nothing ever happens, so editors have to make things up. But that's simply not true. It's just that it's more important for country folks to know the price of corn and calves than the latest crime. They have no need for police reports.

The smaller papers have an unfair advantage; news is more interesting when it's about people you know. In a community newspaper the kid who cut your grass might make the front page, and nothing does so much for the self-esteem as a picture in the local paper. And no matter what kind of a skunk you were in life your home town paper will say something nice about you in your obituary. In a small town weekly the classifieds are not filled with lost souls but lost dogs. Advertisements for yard sales and farm auctions are read carefully because you might want to buy back the stuff you loaned to friends and neighbors over the years.

In the country we are far more interested in our local sports teams than tales about "professionals" who make millions and move around from team to team like transients. Admittedly, a local reporter's objectivity goes out the window when reporting on the home team, but these are our kids and the journalist has to live with these people. There's nowhere to hide.

In a community newspaper the journalism still has a human touch. The editor understands some things are best left unsaid or are none of our business. In a small town you can't write like you're never going to see these people again because tomorrow you will, at the barber shop or the coffee shop where stories are cussed and discussed. In the "Big City," shock jocks and hair sprayed anchors might give us the news fast but in the local newspaper it had better be right or the town's unofficial reporter will set you straight in a letter to the editor.

This may come as a news flash to some of our city cousins but the information superhighway goes down dirt roads too.

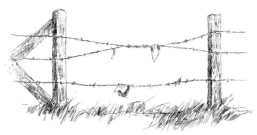

I'M HUNG UP
RIGHT NOW

WHEN IN THE COURSE of human events it becomes necessary to get on the other side of a barbed wire fence there are basically three different techniques: split, straddle and slide.

The slide is the method preferred by sheep, wildflower pickers, hogs, baby calves and kids. The technique is fairly simple to master if you are one of those people who are good at doing the limbo at drunken parties. It means getting down on your belly and sliding under the bottom wire of the fence. I must "point" out that the belly crawl slide is why hogs have short legs, flower pickers have manure on the front of the shirts, why ranch kid's clothes are usually in tatters and why the bottom wire is usually "coated" with previously worn clothing.

If the slide resembles the limbo, the split often resembles another dance step, the twist and shout. Females always think that the grass is greener on the other side of the fence and the split is the technique preferred by women and cows to get there. The split normally requires two people, usually a man and a wife. It is the job of the woman to split the middle wires by standing on the lower one while pulling up on the other, thus creating a window of opportunity for the man. The husband should always go first with the understanding that if the wife lets go of one of the wires while he is in a compromising position the same fate, or worse, could befall her.

I must warn you, if the man happens to let go of one of the rusted wires it could prick the wife's skin bringing forth a few "barbed" comments. It could also cause tetanus and lockjaw but don't let that tempt you.

The straddle is the method preferred by hunters, horses, hikers and bulls. The straddle is performed by pushing down hard on the top wire and hopping over. It should not be performed by men who think they may want to sire children in the near future. The straddle requires a person with a long inseam to avoid having your voice raised three full octaves. Macho men and bulls almost always use the straddle instead of the slide or the split. Thus, the derivation of the old joke, you know, the one about the bull becoming a steer by the time he got to the other side?

Hunters and hikers have developed numerous adaptations to the straddle. These include driving through the fence in a four wheel drive vehicle much like a cow would. Kids and calves go under barbed wire, bulls and men go over and cows and trucks go right through it.

A variation preferred by hunters short of stature is to actually cut the wires. In this case, "twelve gauge" does not refer to the strength of the wire but to the tool used to sever the wires.

If the fence is too tight or the hunter weighs over three hundred pounds the semi-straddle is preferred. This is where the man actually tries to climb the barbed wire fence like it was a ladder. Usually this is done close to a brace so that the hunter has something to hold on to as he brings the full force of his weight to bear on the thread-like wires. Under normal conditions the staples pop out, the wires crumple to the ground and then the hunter can then just walk over the fence.

One precaution that hunters and hikers should take before they get hung up in the straddle position is to make sure the fence is not electrified.

There is one other little known way for getting on the other side of a fence. Although very few people have actually tried this method it can be a simpler and healthier alternative. It is called a gate.

HAVE YOU GOT THE TIME?

FOLKS WHO ATTEND time management seminars, wear wrist watches with three time zones and carry around those cute little binders in which they keep track of every second of every day, can probably tell you that next Tuesday is their spouse's birthday and on Friday they have an appointment with their ulcer doctor. They wouldn't dare be late for their appointment to consult their doctor about "stress," most of which was caused by fidgeting in his waiting room for an hour reading three year old magazines.

Me? I can't tell you what I'm doing this afternoon let alone next week. The batteries in my mantle clock expired last year at exactly 12:30. Since then it's always been "half past" at my house and that's close enough for me. There are not two calendars in my entire home that display the same month; the picture for the month being far more important to me than the fact that the twentieth is a Thursday.

I can remember when we all knew it was Monday, not by a

celebrity calendar, but by the fact that livestock trucks were roaring down Main Street, indicating it was sale day at the auction market. If there was a long line in front of the theater it was Tuesday when the Senior citizens got in for half price. If the parking lot at the church was full you could bet it was "Bingo Wednesday."

You knew the day of the week by the activity planned for the day. Saturday was for taking a bath and Sunday you went to church. These days sinning and filth have become so widespread that churches are open seven days a week and some people actually bathe midweek. At least that's what I'm told.

Both of the media conglomerates aren't helping either. It used to be that you knew it was the Sabbath because Bonanza and Disney's Wonderful World of Color were on TV. Now the Today Show is on tomorrow, USA Today is actually about yesterday and reruns are on every night of the week. Ed Sullivan never missed a Sunday, you could take that to the bank, which by the way, was never open on Saturday.

You could tell the day of the week simply by what was "Closed for Business." Barbers didn't cut hair on Monday and liquor store hours were dictated by blue laws. Back before everything was "super-sized" and chain stores ruled the world, small businesses were often closed one day a week to give the owners a well deserved day off. Now banks are found in all night grocery stores and beer is sold in "We Never Close" gas stations. Which, when you think about it, isn't the greatest idea.

I can remember when Sunday was the only day of the week you dared eat chicken. In fact, you could tell the day of the week just by the menu. In school we knew it was Friday because the school lunchroom served fish in respect to the Catholic faith. Of course, Monday was "hamburger day" at the much dreaded cafeteria. I reached voting age before I discovered there wasn't a law mandating that you eat hamburgers on Monday. Not that it wouldn't be a good law, mind you.

Times really are changing. I can remember when you didn't need a personal digital assistant, or PDA, to indicate the day of rest. You knew because some relatives invariably stopped by after church to interrupt your nap. Now, Sunday is RELATIVELY calm because no one drops in without a scheduled appointment.

It was only a few short decades ago you could survive without wearing a wrist watch. Now folks are managing their time much more wisely, defining each minute, overcrowding every hour and filling in all the squares on every calendar. We have become so busy that when it comes to simply enjoying life we offer up the same excuse a person without a watch used to give …

"Sorry, I haven't got the time."

HAT CHECK

TRUCKERS, RAP SINGERS AND accountants are wearing cowboy hats these days. Stetson is now a cologne and Hollywood beauticians are wearing cowboy hats. Heaven forbid, it's enough to make a real cowboy flip his lid.

Without a government imposed mandatory hat check there are a few simple ways to spot the phonies amongst us. Bright plumage is a sure sign. Real cowboys don't wear feathers in their hats that make them look like pregnant peacocks.

That goes for hat pins too. Anybody who wears a lot of those silver, tie tack looking pins in their hat is probably a collector of convention paraphernalia. If you have brown binding around the outside of your hat brim it is a sure sign you are a cowboy poet.

Hat bands are acceptable as long as they are made out of horse hair. Silver conchas on a hat band indicate you are probably a New York fashion designer.

The hat band of a real cowboy is sweat-stained and dirty.

A word about plastic hat covers. Real cowboys don't cover their hats when it starts raining. Only bankers do this. For gosh sakes, the hat is made from beaver pelt. You know, those animals that swim in water?

If you see someone holding their hat in their hands they probably make their living in the service industries. Cowboys never take off their hats because they know the safest place to keep their hat is on their head. The only time a real cowboy removes his lid is to get a hair cut, and when they are getting shorn they place their hat on its crown so the luck won't fall out. Anyone who lays their hat on its brim on a bed deserves to be shot. Same for the guy who refers to his ten gallon hat as 37.9 liters.

Contrary to what you may think, the color of the hat really doesn't matter as long as it's black or gray. No real cowboy wears a brown hat. Neither does the shape of a person's hat indicate his level of cowboy competence. I've seen a lot of stupid looking hats being worn by some real top hands. Sometimes the shape of a person's hat merely indicates what part of the country he's from. In Texas they wear a low crown and a straight brim. In Utah they wear the back of their hats turned up like they backed into a brick wall.

Nevada buckaroos wear flat brimmed hats with flat crowns. They are tied on with stampede strings or chin cords. Stampede strings are necessary in windy climes and are popular right now with designers and fashion models. Real cowboys install their own chin cords on their hats by getting a rifle shell and striking it with a hammer like a leather punch to make a hole in the hat for the cord to attach. Hopefully this is done with the hat off and the cartridge empty. If not, the deceased probably wasn't a cowboy with much knowledge of munitions.

Arguing about the "best" hat style is like arguing about the best way to cut a sandwich, diagonally or straight across. What really matters are the number of X's in the hat. When John Stetson was building hats there was no hat better than a 5X beaver. Even today there is no standard X rating for hats. So, now we have gas pump jockeys wearing 100 X beavers while I'm wearing a F.B. (factory blemished).

If you have tried to buy a cowboy hat recently you know they all have the name of some famous country western singer welded to a puce or mauve colored hat band. Even though I love country music I don't want anyone's name on my hat but my own. If I wanted to advertise for somebody else I'd wear a free seed corn cap, which, considering the price of hats lately, probably isn't such a bad idea.

GIVE US THIS DAY

THE DAY FINALLY ARRIVED I thought I'd never live to see, the day all the chores were done.

Whatever happened to chores, anyway? Those ceaseless jobs that began and ended each day. We considered them child's work: hauling wood, feeding animals and gathering eggs. The truth was, kids played a vital role in a family's struggle for everyday existence. Now days, big business milks the cow and collects the eggs so that Junior can sleep in, saving energy for a game or a slumber party. We now live in a society where making the bed or doing dishes is child abuse. "Give us this day" is the unspoken prayer of today's youth and that's the problem; they want it given to them, no one wants to work for it.

I'm guessing this theme won't be popular with youngsters who think we've made progress since the days when animals were fed first and a mother could strike fear in young hearts with the simple question, "Are your chores done?" We have sacrificed to give our children a better life but, I wonder, are they better off?

Call me primitive, but I think youth were better educated when they mowed the grass instead of smoked it. When the word "grounded" meant something far different than being sent to a room full of toys. When callouses were a sign of character. Through chores, kids were taught the importance of punctuality by the creatures of habit who waited by the feed trough at the same time every day. Hens didn't lay and cows didn't milk just so kids could take a day off. Kids learned responsibility by milking the cow because, if they didn't, Bossy would explode. Or, so you were told. Drop the eggs and the blame was on your sticky fingers.

Chore children learned to rise early every single day. They gained confidence because they had been trusted with important tasks to perform when no one was watching, like bringing in the wood. Failure to do so meant the whole family froze. I can recall when the words "no allowance" not only referred to what you got paid but the number of mistakes you were permitted. Now youngsters must be "entertained" and are given an allowance just for showing up. Paid for merely bringing home their report card, never mind what's on it. Of course, this was during the stone age when intelligence was not measured solely by B's, C's and PhD's.

I suppose there are reasons why the chores are all done. Burning trash destroys the ozone and eggs now come in cartons. It's not as if a child's life is any easier, survival itself has become a real chore. But by giving our kids cell phones and beepers all we are training them to be are telemarketers, like those who constantly interrupt supper. What else do they know how to do? We never taught them how to work.

They are easily bored and their jeans come pre-ripped because they don't even know how to wear out their pants in the proper places.

Why are we surprised when our grown up children come back home to live? We're the ones who taught them that life is a pyramid scheme, that they could obtain wealth without work. Is it any wonder they grew up allergic to sweat, picking only the low hanging fruit? We gave our children everything except the one thing they needed most, a healthy respect for work. And now we're surprised that they and society aren't working!

We are guilty of child neglect. We neglected to teach that you can't reap what you did not sow. We failed to give our kids a work ethic to fall back on in case they got downsized. If only they knew that no labor was beneath them they could always find a job. Instead, we taught that work should not interfere with pleasure and in so doing we forgot to share one of life's little secrets…the pleasure is in the work.

MY PASSENGERS

D EAR NEPHEW,

I heard you had a little fender bender last week. Thank God you weren't hurt. I know you are expecting this to be a preachy letter from your mean uncle but I'm not ordained to preach. Besides, you've suffered enough already. If not, I'm sure your insurance company will see to that every six months.

You are very special to me and I thought of you a lot during the time I spent in the hospital. I wanted to tell you about a couple girls I met there. Jenna was a bright and beautiful 22 year old passenger in a car driven by her mother-in-law when they were hit by a car with failing brakes. The mother-in-law died and Jenna lived. Some might say that the mother-in-law got the better end of the deal. Her suffering is over.

Jenna has been in the hospital five months now. Every day the bandages that conceal her burns have to be changed twice by angels in tennis shoes, the nurses. Jenna's burns will hopefully heal someday if the doctors can just get rid of the staph infection. But poor Jenna will never have the use of her legs again, they were both amputated above the knee.

I received the loveliest letter from Jenna's mother. What a courageous woman. She wanted to know if I could use the liquid supplement they had left because Jenna can now eat hospital food. As if that's a great improvement!

I never did learn the name of the other girl who kicked me out of my private room. I was glad to give it to her because she had just spent eight days in Intensive Care fighting for her life. Daily, as I hobbled down the hallway, I saw her sitting in a wheelchair surrounded by her many friends. Looking beyond the bandages you could tell this eighteen year old had once been a real beauty and very popular.

She too had been a passenger in an automobile when the driver lost control and the car rolled over and over. Some very brave people stopped her from being burned to death but not before her lungs filled with smoke and chemical retardant from the fire extinguishers. I'm told she got hit in the head by a tree branch but hopefully there will be no permanent brain damage, just endless reconstructive surgeries. I can tell you from personal experience that one operation is one too many.

I nodded to the young girl as I passed her room but she could not talk as her jaw was wired shut. At night I heard her crying and moaning. The shots, pills nor the morphine pump could mask the pain. I don't think it was any less painful for the parents and relatives. Every day I saw them in the patio outside my room as they stared into the blackness of their countless coffee cups. For them, visiting hours were twenty four hours every day. How difficult it must be for a parent to see their child suffer such pain. I'd think it is an experience from which there would be no recovery. Can you imagine how the other driver must feel?

It haunts me that one minute these two beautiful girls were enjoying life with a clear and straight road in front of them and the next minute their lives were horribly altered. Forever. And through no fault of their own. Yes, these two young ladies left a lasting impression on me.

I have started driving again after surgery but it's not the same. I am a changed driver. I'm not in such a hurry any more, I try to be more courteous and if someone raises a middle finger at me for going too slow I just smile and glance in my rear view mirror. There I see the two faces of the girls I met in the hospital. Objects in the mirror really are bigger than they appear.

Those two faces in the mirror remind me that even though I may be the only one in the car we always carry passengers with us.

STUFF I DON'T NEED

CALL ME A CURMUDGEON, if you must, but I think our lives might possibly be enhanced if we could just get rid of a few things that we don't really need but can't seem to live without. Besides cluttering up our three-car garages, they clutter up our lives as well. In an effort to simplify my life I compiled a list of some of the stuff in our modern society that I can easily live without.

This may come as a surprise to some but my life would change very little without state lotteries, hemorrhoid and feminine hygiene advertisements on television, leveraged buyouts, call waiting, modern art and car alarms that go off during my nap at the slightest provocation and for no apparent reason.

I consider my library complete without a single book written by a murderer, his lawyer or tell-all girl friend.

Perhaps I should be ashamed to admit that I do not own a single silk tie, pair of designer jeans or a wrist watch that cost more than some families make in an entire year.

I find that I can easily live without a diamond earring in my ear or the few hairs I have left wrapped in a rubber band and made to look like a pony tail. I don't need a wife with a tattoo, a hyphenated last name or a pierced eye lid, navel or nostril. I find life a lot simpler without glitz, greed and glitter .

Have the following items really made this a better place to live? Gas-powered leaf blowers, IRS forms, electric wrenches, violent computer games, 25-inch stereo speakers mounted in the back of small pickups, ballpoint pens that write upside down, television sets with 200 channels and rap music?

I don't need to stay in a $250-per-night hotel room with carpet on the walls and a fern bar in the lobby to sleep well at night. My conscience is clear.

There are some people who I don't want cluttering up my life either. These would include flag burners, doomsday environmentalists, television preachers, animal rights terrorists, mid-afternoon talk show hosts, the British Royalty, door-to-door salesmen peddling religion, psychoanalysts, debutantes, adulterers, phone solicitors and militant vegetarians. I don't tell them how to live their lives and would appreciate the same courtesy.

Couldn't we all get along without assault rifles, corporate welfare, news fakers, tyrannical employees of government agencies, air you can see and chemicals you can't, $1,000-per-plate dinners, Political Action Committees, taxpayer-subsidized chauffeur-driven limousines, first-class airline seats and valet parking?

There may be something missing in my life but I'm pretty sure it's not quiche, caviar, tofu, soy burgers, sun dried tomatoes, brie or buck a bottle water.

Surely the world would not come to an end tomorrow without junk mail, tanning salons, speed trap radar, porno movies, pin striping, car phone faxes and cats and dogs with more clothes than children who live in third world countries.

I could live in a world quite comfortably without pushy crowds, AIDS, drunk drivers, breast cancer and racism.

It seems to me that this old world of ours might be a more comfortable place to live if some of us would make a list of things we could live without instead of a long shopping list of stuff that only serves to complicate our lives.

SACRED COWS

I FIND IT FRIGHTENING that baby boomers may be the first generation in our nation's history who have collectively never milked a cow. That fact alone is responsible for a culture of milquetoast handshakes, spoiled kids and consumers who have no idea where their food comes from. Sadly, we live in a society that criticizes the cow while cutting the cheese.

These days, choreless city kids sit on their duffs and tell their parents, "Don't have a cow." And Mom and Dad take it literally. It seems no one keeps a cow anymore.

In days past, when we stored the milk in the cow instead of the refrigerator, milking began and ended each day. A farm kid who grew up far from the convenience store was the closest thing a family had to a "milking machine." Such a child learned valuable lessons from old Bossy; that five o'clock came twice in the same 24-hour period, that you should keep your mouth shut while working and that you should never approach anything from the rear. A child who milked learned important things, like responsibility, and how to shoot a milky stream into the cat's mouth from a distance of ten feet. Those who milked seldom partied all night.

The chores of the modern day child consist of turning the TV off and the air conditioner on. Kids think the basic food groups are the can, the bottle and the fast food drive-up window. They are under the impression that milk expires according to a date on a carton. A farm kid knew that milk expired when the family cow did and so they took good care of her. In the "days of dairy" a child could learn as much by sticking his head into the flank of a cow as between the covers of a book. But now we have urban bred teachers who ask stupid questions, such as, "How much milk does a cow give?" Any well educated farm kid knows that a cow doesn't GIVE you anything. You have to go and get it at the most inconvenient times.

In a simpler era you could easily identify those who had grown up sitting on a milk stool by shaking their hand. It's not something you can fake, lie about or water down. Either you have drained a cow's crankcase or you haven't. You'd better not lie about it because you may be asked to do it, and just like opening a modern day milk carton, it requires a certain knack that takes time to master.

When Bossy was BOSS the cow was an honored member of the family. We thanked God for our daily bread and the cow for freshly squeezed milk. Now an entire generation thinks ice cream comes from two aging hippies named Ben and Jerry. The new and improved, industrial strength cow is milked for all she's worth, and forced to give up her calf so that an ungrateful human may bottle feed their child and not be inconvenienced. The cow gets credit only for global warming and hardened arteries.

The family milk cow has been replaced by 2,000 head dairies where we let others do our milking for us. The result is that there are 2,000 more kids who sleep late every morning. Butter has been replaced by oleomargarine, our milk shakes contain no milk, exercise substitutes for hard work and politicians substitute for real leaders. We elect bureaucrats who know how to milk a taxpayer but not a cow. And we send our kids off to teachers who don't know which end of the cow the hay goes in, who don't know how many faucets a cow has or how to turn them on. But they are telling our kids how the cow ate the cabbage.

Personally, I don't consider any person truly educated unless they have tried to coax a little mother's milk from the udder of one of God's greatest creatures in the early morning darkness.

HO HO HOBO

'TWAS THE NIGHT BEFORE Christmas and the family was en route to grandma's house. As they motored through the intersection of a small sleepy town the ill mannered child in the back seat yelled into his father's ear, "It's him, it's him, it's Santa Claus."

There on the curb was a forlorn looking fellow with a dirty white beard, a stocking cap that barely covered his head and a red tattered coat that was frayed white around the edges.

The parents glanced at the ragged man with all his possessions sitting next to him in a plastic grocery bag. "You have to admit," said the mother, "he does look like Santa with his scuffed up old boots and his matted beard."

"Don't be silly, he's just a ho, ho hobo," laughed the father. "The only thing that transient has in common with Santa is he probably only works one day a year."

But the ill mannered child was throwing a tantrum in the back seat. "I want to stop and see Santa!"

"He looks more like Santa than those photocopies back home," said the mother as the car rolled to a stop and the kid escaped out the back door.

"Hi Santa," said the child, shocking the jolly old gent out of his quiet reverie. Despite his age the old man was quick to catch on. With the parents looking a bit apprehensive, the old man pulled the young boy up on one knee of his dirty old pants. Before the homeless man realized what was happening the child was listing the presents he expected to find the very next morning under the Christmas tree.

"I want a joy stick, a bike and a laser gun." The old man had never heard of many of the toys the boy rattled off. "My sister wants a baby that drinks, wets and cries. Daddy wants a new table saw and mommy wants a fur coat. But you already know all that because I sent you a letter. You got it didn't you?"

The old man didn't know what to say and just nodded his head. He hadn't spoken to a child or held one on his lap for many years.

"I have to warn you," said the boy to the smiling Santa, "Grandma doesn't have a chimney so we'll have to leave the front door unlocked for you."

The parents looked sick as they shared a vision of this bum walking through an open door and stealing all their presents. "Come on son, we have to be going now."

"Maybe you better write this down so you don't forget it all," said the son to Santa, ignoring his parents as usual.

Before putting the boy down the old man reached into his sack for something to give the child, but there was nothing in the sack but dirty clothes. There was a tear in the old man's eye as he reached to his neck and took off a gold chain with a golden cross with the figure of Jesus attached. He had worn the crucifix for as long as he could remember. A reminder of better times. He gave that small boy the only possession he owned that was worth anything. "You keep this present and do what your mom and dad tell you, and whenever you need some extra help in life you just grab hold of this cross and pray for good things."

The parents looked grateful and sad, and then realized they had a lot of shopping to do before the next morning if they were to acquire all the presents on their child's wish list. They waved good-bye to the old man who lived out of a sack.

Once they were back in the car the young boy told his dad, "That was the best Santa of all."

Years later the youngster had children of his own. At about the age of six, one by one, his kids would ask, "Dad is there really a Santa Claus?" He would clasp the gold crucifix he wore close to his heart and reply, "Yes there is. I met him in person."

NEIGHBORIN'

THE ART OF NEIGHBORIN' is a concept foreign to most city folks. Urbanites can live beside each other for years without ever sharing pie or its recipe. The folks next door are just people to keep up with. It's not even called a neighborhood any more, it's "the hood." Although that is more apt to describe the residents therein.

In fairness, being a good neighbor in the country is easier simply because of space. The distance buffers the piano lessons, fire crackers, barking dogs and family spats. But even though you can't hear your friends fight through a thin wall you can eavesdrop just by sending the kids over to play for the day.

Country folk don't borrow sugar much. They are more apt to borrow water when the well runs dry or milk when the cow does. Neighbors think nothing of borrowing a tractor. But even the best machine can't replace a good neighbor.

Folks in the country "lived together" before that meant what it does now. Out of necessity if nothing else. When it came time to brand the calves there were never enough competent ropers so ranchers traded help. Even today, there still aren't enough good "heelers" if you don't count the dogs. In the country we live by the honor system where wayward calves and kids are shown the way home. A good neighbor admires your cattle, and says so, but he doesn't steal them.

Country folk have a long standing tradition of helping one another. Before there were phones when someone got sick a neighbor would tell a neighbor and so on down the line until the doctor was found. What started out as scarlet fever became a difficult child birth by the time the doctor was told. If he was too late in arriving you were buried in a community cemetery. Laid to rest amongst friends and relatives. If your barn burned down a new one would be raised and if for some reason you couldn't harvest your crop a neighbor would do it for you. You didn't need food stamps because the neighbors had a garden.

Still today, if there's an emergency it's probably the phone next door that rings, not 911. Even if "next door" is three miles away. When a coyote or a bureaucrat is prowling the neighborhood a good neighbor will send up a modern day smoke signal.

A neighbor might call to inform you that you DID HAVE a water trough overflowing or a hard calving cow. Notice the past tense. It's not a problem any more because the neighbor just happened to be in the neighborhood and took care of the problem.

The key to being a good neighbor is courtesy. (There's a word you don't hear much any more.) It means you don't run your bulls next to your neighbor's heifers. If your beloved dog has become a nuisance in the neighborhood you get rid of it. If some fool starts a fire on your place you light a back fire and burn your valuable grass so the fire won't spread to your neighbor next door. Because they'd do the same for you.

To an urban dweller this may all seem like strange behavior for folks who are actually competitors, producing the same product, like two fast food joints on opposite sides of the intersection. But we don't look at it that way. Good neighbors would rather have your friendship than your money.

When city folk escape to the country, neighborin' is the first thing they should learn. But they don't. Instead they build a big fence and get a mean dog. They might as well have stayed in town because neighbors are what make the country a decent place to live. In the country we realize if everyone just treated the folks next door a little better, the rest of the world would take care of itself.

NEVER SLEEP NAKED

Normally, I am of the opinion that what a person does in his own bed is his own business. But when that behavior is dangerous and offensive to others I feel a need to speak out. I am referring to people who sleep uncovered, and I am not alluding to sheets, blankets and comforters. I am talking about people who sleep divested of their clothing ... in the buff ... naked as a jaybird!

To someone like me who sleeps in his flannel "jammies" every night such conduct is despicable. If God had wanted us to sleep stark naked he would have made our bodies better looking and never would have blessed us with frilly, see through lingerie. Besides, sleeping in the natural state can be extremely dangerous, as Don can tell you.

Don was sleeping as he does every night, fully exposed, when he was jarred awake by the loud barking of his dogs. His three dogs were making the most annoying racket, even more so than usual. So,

Don pulled himself out of bed to see what was causing their displeasure. Don was shirtless, coatless and had pants to match. On his way out of the house he didn't even bother to throw on a robe. To you and me, making a spectacle of oneself by appearing in the nude would be considered deviant behavior. Evidently, to the residents of a certain small town in Oregon it is quite a normal occurrence.

For some reason Don's dogs were clear across the road, looking back at the house from a safe distance. Howling at the top of their lungs. This was very strange behavior for the dogs who usually never strayed too far from their prostrate position under the house. Looking slightly to his left, Don saw the reason that the dogs had distanced themselves from the porch. Standing there was the fattest member of the "spiny pig" family that Don had ever seen. It was when Don first made eye contact with the porcupine that it first dawned on him that prancing about, stripped of accouterments, might not be conducive to good health. You could catch a cold… among other things.

I am told that in their normal state a porcupine's quills lay down next to the body until the animal becomes excited. Then they stand at attention. The quills have barbs on them like fish hooks that pull themselves ever so gently, deeper and deeper into the flesh. I am also informed that it's quite painful to be zapped by a porcupine. It is a common misconception, however, that porcupines can "shoot" their quills as if from a gun. This is simply not true. Usually they try to brush you with their tail and their maximum range is actually less than three feet.

Unfortunately for Don, he was standing well within that range. And the porcupine's quills were standing at attention, poised for attack. Generally, it can be said that porcupines are rather slow and stupid, although, I would never say that to a porcupine's face. But this porcupine must have been the Albert Einstein of the porcupine community, because when Don slowly turned to go into his house to fetch a rifle, and perhaps put on some pants, the porcupine immediately sensed the danger. Either that or the sight of Don's ugly body in the moonlight just scared the poor beast into action. Whatever the cause, the porcupine fired first.

Don let out a howl that even scared the dogs. Needless to say, Don was unable to retrieve his gun, get dressed or even go back to sleep. For quite some time I am told.

I report this true story as a public service for those disgusting people who, like Don, go to bed in their birthday suits every night. This is not just a tall tale intended for entertainment purposes. I assure you that Don's encounter makes a point in the end. Which is exactly where the quills landed, according to paramedics on duty that night.

LOST IN AMERICA

To quote a poet, "Two roads diverged in a yellow wood." One route took the high road while the other led down the wrong path. Today, in America two roads diverge. One is a detour and the other is a dead end. The signposts have all been taken down and the meandering path through modern life is constantly under construction. America has lost its way, and just like a stubborn husband at the wheel, we refuse to ask for directions. Americans have no idea where their food is grown, where their next meal is coming from or where their kids are at the moment.

Our landmarks have been remodeled, homogenized and turned into tourist traps. Yes, we are lost, but we're still in a hurry. Without even the time to stop and say good-bye to old friends. We eat in fast food restaurants that don't have the time to do anything "well done" and we shop in malls so large we can't find our cars in the parking lot. But America is alive and well, even if we are growing morally bankrupt.

On the road of life we are stalled on the shoulder of the highway, and no one will stop to help out. We'd phone home but what's the point? There wouldn't be anyone there. The kids are at day care and mom and pop are both working to give their kids all the things they never had. Like assault weapons, AIDS and crack cocaine.

Gone are the guideposts that used to direct us. History books are being rewritten and tradition is something to apologize for. Lawyers debate the "economics of ethics" and "spin doctors" prescribe a liberal dose of deception. It's hard to be loyal to the home team with athletes changing sides as often as they change socks. "Anything for a buck," is quickly becoming our nation's new motto.

We used to rely on morals, ethics and religion to show us the way. In God we trusted. But God doesn't have a page on the Internet and with 200 TV channels we can't keep track which station our minister is on. Oh well, it was becoming difficult to tell the difference between the TV preacher and the Home Shopping Network anyway. Rules and laws used to keep us on the right course but our ethical compass is broken and our moral map has been folded and mutilated beyond recognition. The old laws no longer apply. Violence is accepted as long as you have a good jump shot, fast ball or a team of high profile lawyers on your side.

Don't look for guidance in the written or spoken word. Gone are the trusted voices of Erma Bombeck, James Herriot and Will Rogers. Country music is now sung by rockers in black hats who never set foot outside the city limits. Best selling books are scribbled by celebrities whose characters don't have any; character that is. Can you imagine any of the bestsellers written by defense attorneys, spoiled athletes or dethroned politicians being read as classics 100 years from now? For that matter, will anyone be watching reruns of the trash currently on television or humming the words to the latest rap music hit? We can only hope not.

Thanks to political correctness we don't even speak the same language any more in this country. *Please, no thank you* and *take my seat* are seldom heard and the only four letter words you shouldn't utter are work, cook, love and read. A wedding invitation might be addressed to Mister and Misses, Ms and Mister or Mister and Mister. Today's toys for all ages come with instructions written in four languages and even the English is indecipherable for the "intellectually challenged."

Yes, we are lost far from home and searching for direction. I don't know if we will find ourselves but if we continue on the path we are traveling I'm sure we are going to be disappointed when we get to wherever it is we think we are going.

THE FLAG IS UP

WE'VE GONE FROM the Pony Express to e-mail and we are wired by telephone, satellite dish and computer modem, yet a little old mailbox remains our primary link to the outside world.

We call them boxes but they're not really. Receptacle is probably a better description but a much more unfriendly word. A good mailbox should be friendly if nothing else. When a check, gift or letter arrives a mailbox could more aptly be described as a treasure chest.

They come in all shapes, sizes and colors: white, black or rusty. They sit precariously on crooked wooden posts, pieces of pipe welded to an old disc blade, links of chain or horseshoes welded together. The occasional dull post hole auger can even be spotted holding up a rectangular receptacle. Mailboxes just seem to bring out the creativity in a person.

Some are more ornamental than useful, complete with roofs and windows. They are works of art. I've seen mailboxes made in the shape of barns, houses and even the occasional pot bellied stove, and others so homely a bird wouldn't roost on them. You'll probably notice, if you bother to look, that ugly mailboxes usually don't have the name of the resident painted on the side, just a faded number. Some folks are too ashamed of their mailbox to put their name on it.

A mailbox is a reflection of the box holder's personality. They define who we are. I've seen a wine barrel used as a mailbox for a winery and a Holstein cow collecting mail for a dairy. It takes a pretty smart mailman to figure out the right combination to a cow. Does he pull on the leg, the head or the tail to open it?

Speaking of combinations, folks in the country don't have to lock their mailboxes like city dwellers do. And our mailboxes aren't stacked on top of each other like the people who live inside a condominium complex. Country mailboxes usually stand in solitary silence awaiting the mailman. Either that or a group of mailboxes will stand at the end of a dirt road. Even then no two are alike.

Although you bought and paid for your own mailbox and planted it on your own land, it is the property of the United States Postal Service. No one but the postman can legally put anything inside. Even the weekly newspaper must have its own repository. The teenage prankster, who puts a dead snake inside your mailbox to scare the wits out of you, could be arrested for mail fraud.

I pity the people who have a postal box in a big city post office and have to wait in a long line. Or, pay a store front business to rent a box. I've got news for those people, there is no monthly charge for a good old fashioned mailbox at the side of the road. I think folks who go to town to pick up their mail just want a more prestigious address than their real one.

The mailbox can make or break an entire day. The worst feeling in the world is to see that the red flag is down, meaning the postman has come, and going to the mailbox only to find it empty. Not even a bill. "Empty" pretty much describes the feeling of knowing that not even the junk mailers cared enough to send you some mail today. Of course, the best feeling in the world is to get a package so big it wouldn't fit inside the box and had to be tied on the outside.

Now that we're faxing and e-mailing each other, selling stuff on satellite and country kids are going to school in front of a computer instead of taking a correspondence course, I suppose the mailbox will become less important in our daily lives. Somehow, I just don't think an electronic mailbox will be quite the same.

FAIR TIME IS FUN TIME

I'T'S SUMMER TIME and that can mean only one thing; all over the country parents are using up their valuable vacation time to chaperone their 4-H or FFA child at the county fair. No, that's not entirely correct. Parents are using up their precious vacation to babysit their child's project animal while their offspring is acquiring valuable life experiences on the carnival midway.

As a fair parent you have three options: (#1) You could spend three hours a day commuting to the fair and two hours looking for a parking place. Of course, while you are commuting your child will be entertaining himself by tossing quarters into ash trays, getting sick on wild carnival rides or making arrangements to run away with their newest role model. (#2) You could live in a camper for six days without running water. (#3) You could stay in a motel room for $100 a night and feed your family a steady diet of cinnamon rolls, corn dogs and lemonade.

Staying on the fairgrounds is probably your best option because the "fair mother" is going to be on constant call to fluff up the tails of steers or to wash manure stains out of white show pants on a regular basis. For six days you will be cussing the individual who came up with the idea of wearing white pants and a white shirt as a show uniform to exhibit an animal that is covered in hair spray, shoe polish and recycled hay.

Unfortunately, the ribbons are handed out at the start of the week. This means that after your child finishes dead last in the show ring you will have the rest of the week to feel humiliated in front of the other parents. You've spent four months living with this animal and you were unlucky enough to get an idiot for a judge! You plead with your child, "Please stop crying. Here's $20, go play on the bungee jump."

Now, let's see. Your child finished last in class and in the showmanship contest the animal broke away and toppled over the Cattlewomen's by-product display. Oh well, there's always the clean stall award! So for the next five days you get up at five A.M. to make sure the lamb has clean straw and there are no "hot ones" behind the steers. You are beginning to look seedy but the pig has its hair combed and powdered.

It's 110 degrees in the shade and you find yourself becoming jealous of a steer because it has a fan and a mister and you don't. All you want to do is go home, take a shower, sleep in your own bed and forget about the fact that the hog is not eating, the steer is not drinking or the lamb is not breathing.

Boredom sets in. After all, you can only look at the displays of relief maps made from seven kinds of beans so many times. The food display stopped looking appetizing long ago. That cake may have been worthy of a blue ribbon ten days ago but not now that the sugar has petrified. You worry about your mental health when the highlight of your day is listening to the sales pitch of the slice and dice salesman in the big tent.

At last the big moment arrives ... sale day. Your child is ecstatic that he got four dollars a pound for his lamb which won't even come close to paying for the motel bill for the week. But your child thinks it was a highly profitable enterprise. Oh well, the fair was an educational experience. Yeah, right! Now you have a kid that wants to grow up and be a demolition derby driver, a pig racer, or carve wood signs for a living. That's probably all right though, because the fact that he won the clean stall award probably won't be enough to get him into Stanford or Yale.

Finally, it is time to leave the fair and the project animal behind. For the next six weeks your child won't speak to you because you didn't buy back the project animal and make it a permanent member of the family. What a mean person you are!

THE PEDIGREE OF MAN

THE PAST CAME ALIVE on the wall of my grandparent's house. Gazing down with stern stares from photos were five generations of my family. As a child those people scared me to death. One old geezer looked particularly mean but I suppose I would too if I lived in a sod house with a woman as cranky looking as my great-great-grandma. I've seen prettier faces in a hackamore.

There wasn't a lot of pageantry in the past. The men wore dark suits, shaggy beards and dour sneers. It's obvious I come from a long line of men who resembled gnarled cedar roots, and the women weren't much prettier. They wore high necked dresses, cameos and appeared upset because the husband was the only one who got to sit down for the photo shoot.

The pictures weren't actually photographs but tin types, images etched in metal. We were lucky to have them and only did so because my great-great-grandpa was a photographer/undertaker.

To no avail, he probably said to his undertaking clients, "Smile and say cheese."

I've always felt that the pedigree of man is not important, other than the fact that if these folks weren't born we would still be swimming around the gene pool. We shouldn't place emphasis on ancestry, because, these days a child might be the result of a conjugal visit or may not even know a parent, let alone a grandparent.

I hate to admit this but I couldn't tell you the name of several of those ancestors on my grandparent's wall. This from a fellow who would require a bull to have an impressive five generation pedigree before being allowed to mingle with my cows. Interestingly, we know more about the ancestry of a range ram or a lap dog than we do ourselves. We know more about the family of a race horse than we do its owners.

I'm not suggesting that people should be culled like farm animals on the basis of their bloodlines or evaluated on the performance of their ancestors as if they were horses. People should never be judged by their parents. Progeny are not better simply because of their last name or because they are trust fund beneficiaries. If you are of superior stock then prove it on your own. Nor should citizens be condemned for life for some "bad blood" flowing in their veins. We are all pedigreed stock.

Don't get me wrong, I definitely don't want our old world back, but you can preserve the past without living in it. Every family should have a recorded history because at some point most everyone is interested in discovering where they came from. No doubt, you'll be disappointed to discover that some branches of your family tree either did not branch or should have been pruned. It's quite possible that great-great-great-grandpa wasn't all that "great." He might have been a robber baron, ordered your great-great-great grandma from a catalog like a plow or was buried in a shallow grave on Boot Hill. There's no need to apologize. I myself am told that I have a dead relative who was a lawyer, but I am assured it was "relatively" distant.

The family histories that I've read are better than most books that litter our best seller lists. These ancient accounts help explain why a family has voted Democratic since Jefferson, why certain family members are still feuding and where an embarrassing middle name originated. It's comforting to imbibe occasionally on a bit of nostalgia and be able to put a face with a family heirloom, an antique or a tombstone.

I remembered those old pictures on my grandparents wall when it dawned on me that I am the last of my line. This branch of the family tree did not bud. I realized that a hundred years from now some little kid is NOT going to look up and see my gnarled, ugly face on the wall and get scared to death.

MECHANICAL BULL

THE DIFFERENCE BETWEEN FARMERS and ranchers is mostly mechanical. Your typical farmer belongs to the "Tool Of The Month Club" and has a 14 drawer tool chest stuffed with an assortment of pliers and punches. The rancher, on the other hand, owns one tool, a pair of all-in-one fence pliers. One size fits all. Take away the rancher's duct tape and baling wire and he wouldn't know how to fix a thing.

A farmer believes everything can be fixed with a squirt of oil; whereas, the rancher thinks the world's problems can be solved with a shot of antibiotic. The farmer tracks grease on the carpet, the rancher leaves footprints of muck. To a rancher a Phillips screwdriver is an alcoholic beverage that cures constipation.

Farmers and ranchers look at life through different safety goggles. Filling up with gas is as mechanical as a rancher wants to get and a flat tire calls for Triple AAA®. He would rather rope the stock than put them through an iron chute and his backside fits a saddle but will not conform to a tractor seat. He leaves the gooseneck hooked to the truck permanently because he finally got the blinker lights to correspond to the turn indicators. When fixing a float valve he tells the wife, "Don't force it just get a bigger hammer."

A hole in the fence to a farmer is an invitation for cattle to get into his corn and an opportunity to fire up the arc welder and start stringing sucker rod. The rancher sticks his wife in the gap and tells her to flap her arms up and down to scare the stock away.

When a farm kid takes an aptitude test the results indicate he should become an engineer, mechanic or enroll in "tool school." He grows up overhauling engines and taking apart toys to see how they work. But the hands of a ranch kid won't fit a wrench. The tools of his trade are the rope and saddle. If you had to change the oil on a horse a cowboy would never get out of the corral. If cows had grease fittings we'd all be vegetarians! The cattleman has to hire someone just to nail shoes on his horse's feet and couldn't pound a nail into a snow bank if he had to. The extent of his mechanical experience is limited to changing the batteries in a flash light. The rancher doesn't know a carburetor from a Corriente.

Likewise, the farmer has no idea which end of the cow kicks. He routinely forgets to feed the dog and would view a difficult calving as an opportunity to use the PTO on a tractor. To a farmer a "Deere" and a "Cat" are cherished and much respected pieces of farm equipment. To a rancher they are animals to be shooed away.

Farmers and ranchers are "threaded" differently. A farmer wears steel toed lace up boots and coveralls. If he forgets his name it's stenciled on his pocket. A rancher wouldn't be caught dead in overalls with a shop rag in his pocket. In the farmer's shop you will find a calendar of pretty girls holding big pipe wrenches and bins of sorted screws. The rancher feels at home in the tack room with the smell of wet saddle blankets and the absence of anything made of steel. He prefers leather because it doesn't rust. His calendar has cows on it.

A few folks have tried to blend both cultures. Dairymen know about animals and tools and thus are considered "uppity" by both farmers and ranchers. On any big ranch the least respected employee is the windmill man because mechanically inclined stockman have always been considered about "half a bubble off" by the rest of us.

WHEN WE GROW UP

SHAME ON US! We ought to be sent to our room without supper or made to sit in a corner with a dunce cap. It doesn't matter that we are going morally bankrupt as long as there's a new car in the garage and the economy is fine. But the good times will end with the next recession and we'll still be minus our morals.

We have failed in our most important job, as role models to the next generation. Life is a journey made easier by sign posts along the way, left by those who have gone before to make the journey easier for those who follow. But our generation has left no such sign posts, leaving our kids to wander aimlessly in the mall. Ask a kindergartner or a college student what they want to be when they grow up and you'll get a blank stare and a shrug. As parents we spent all our time at work or at the gym to buff up our bodies or the bottom line, but look in the mirror and you may not see anything of substance. If youngsters want to find a hero these days they must tune into a

Saturday morning cartoon show.

As a kid I wanted to be a professional baseball or basketball player; although, I couldn't even dunk a donut properly, let alone a basketball. But we had our heroes, didn't we? These days what is there to emulate? Athletes who bite ears, strangle coaches, do drugs and molest young girls. But it's all right as long as you announce that you are not a "role model." You can be "as bad as you wannabe" just as long as you can rebound well.

If you are keeping score the mess is everywhere. Actors and actresses testify in Congress about righteous things and then appear in movies smoking cigarettes, doing drugs and mowing down people with guns. Rap singers rhapsodize about killing people. What has happened to the idea that the good guys were supposed to win? That we should strive to be better?

As children, my generation alternately wanted to be firemen, teachers, policemen or doctors. You'd have to be crazy to aspire to such heights now. Teachers and firemen get shot on the job, doctors get sued or HMO'ed and the media investigates the cops more than the criminals. It used to be that the ultimate goal was to grow up to be President. But now it is for different reasons. According to the media, the Presidency seems like a good place to meet women. Talk about your role models! These reporters long ago gave up on being accurate, let alone ethical. The moral code of the tabloid journalists is determined by Nielsen Ratings and opinion surveys. I don't know which is more honest, members of the World Wrestling Federation or Hollywood defense attorneys defending lewd behavior.

The place where we have really failed is in the home at our most important task. The kids are sent off to be raised by day care and if they misbehave they are put on drugs, just like their parents. The message we are sending is, it's all right to cheat on your spouse as long as you don't get caught. What you do in your own house or with your own life is nobody's business, which means you can go on leading a decadent life because no one is watching. Kids no longer look UP to grownups but DOWN on us. The only role model we are providing is how NOT to act.

In this void kids are turning more to inanimate objects, like computers, for direction. Perhaps, it's just as well. Computers don't lie, batter their mother and are usually around when they are needed. But by failing to provide the next generation with role models and heroes we are also stealing our children's hopes, goals and dreams.

No one should have the right to do that to a child.

GOOD NIGHT

I HEAR THAT ARCHITECTS ARE putting porches back on houses these days, although they have no idea why. Mostly for decoration, I'd say. Country folks know why; because, when the day is worn out, and so are they, the porch is the best seat in the house. You don't have to buy a ticket or a new dress to see a sunset.

I'm not sure that porches will work in the big city. It's just too darn noisy. Besides, you're a better target for a drive-by shooting. Sunset is supposed to be the hour of calm but city sounds are so unsettling. Car alarms go off constantly, grating on the nerves like a chain saw on a pipe, but nobody pays any attention, so the burglars are free to do their after hours shopping under the cover of darkness. Back fire, gun fire, a scream in the dead of night. Literally.

When the rural sun sets at least you can see it. In the city when the sun and moon trade places a clear moonlit night may be obliterated by tall buildings and bad air that is not fit to breathe. Better go hide in the house.

Porch sitters know that no matter how bad the day, a good night can still save it. Nighttime reminds us that there are degrees of darkness. As the sun sets our spirits rise, but in the city the night can actually be more stressful than the day. Citified sunsets are filled with sounds of neighbors fighting, planes landing, beepers beeping, phones ringing, cars leaving rubber and trucks leaving town. Blaring boom boxes belt out music that would drive a howling wolf to suicide.

Beyond the city limits, nature makes the music if there's any to be made. A calf calls for its mom, she answers back and you can almost hear them pairing up. If only it were so in the city.

Country stillness is audible. Wind rustles through the trees, hoot owls give a hoot, lambs bawl and bugs buzz. Crickets chirp rather than talking heads on television. Inside, a weather man warns about the threat of rain, while outside the coyote's report is more reliable. If the coyote wails, it's going to pour, a shout and it will be dry. But you have to be wise enough to know the difference.

The rocking chair is still the best place to fall asleep during the decline of the day. But urban bedclothes are not made for parading on the porch. Thirsty mosquitoes find perfume and skimpy night gear very enticing, even if your husband does not. Which brings up another point I'd like to discuss. Evening porch time used to be for courtin' but we have somehow skipped that phase of falling in love. Too bad too, for those were the best hours of our lives.

City folks are always worried about their "night life." But it really isn't necessary to be doing anything when the country air is being let out of the day. Evenings were made for solitude, cud chewing, swatting bugs, whittling, crocheting, cooling off and winding down. Conversation is usually limited to grunts and yawns. We just natu- rally know when it's time for bed, we don't need a curfew.

Missing sunsets is not their fault, I guess. City folks have to live where there's a living. But sometimes I wonder if inner peace wouldn't be just as good as a bigger piece of the pie? When the sun and moon are fighting for control of the light switch, and tomorrow is turning into today, the sunset reminds us all that this day is gone forever. We take it for granted that the sun is shining on the other side of night but we ought to be enjoying life like this was our last sunset.

Go sit on the porch. Someday it will be.

IS ANYBODY THERE?

G<small>O AHEAD</small>, call me old fash-
ioned but I refuse to use an ATM machine. I tore up the ATM card
they gave me, preferring to do business with the teller I have known
for twenty years. Recently, I got a notice from the bank informing me
that in the future they are going to charge me for each bank transac-
tion if I actually want to talk to a teller. However, the ATM machine
will be free. The bank is trying to force me to enter the computer age.

It's the same everywhere. We now use credit card gas pumps
which give real meaning to the words, "self service." And I am told
there are prototype grocery stores where you simply push your fully
loaded cart of groceries through an airport security-like device and
the computer tells you how much your bank account will be automatically debited. Of course this will put a lot of people out of work,
but the computers are doing real well.

What makes all this possible are bar codes. Before too long I think
all babies will be bar coded at birth on their foreheads so we can do

away with credit cards.

It dawned on me just how far we've come down the information highway when I checked into a hotel room recently in a big city. When I called and made a reservation they took my credit card number. When I arrived I was instructed by a sign to go straight to room #315, swipe my credit card in the mini-computer on the door and the door would unlock and all charges applied to my credit card bill. From the way the bed was made up I think they had a computer do that too.

Needless to say, I am having a difficult time adjusting to all this. After I was settled in the hotel room I called the front desk to request a wake up call. Right on time the next morning a pleasant voice said, "Good morning this is your wake up call." Being the polite person that I am, I replied, "Thank you very much." After fully waking up I realized that I had just said *thank you* to a computer who couldn't understand a word I said. Or maybe it could, they are making them very smart these days.

I ordered a burger at a fast food drive-up the other day and a computer clown thanked me, although it did sound rather hollow and insincere. The toll taker at the bridge has been replaced by a basket that counts change and I'm told they now have a computer that catches you speeding and mails you a ticket. The very thought of no more highway patrolmen must send shivers down the spine of anyone who owns a donut shop.

I was sitting in my recliner the other night browsing on television when the phone rang. I am sad to report that big business has now discovered the perfect salesman. One who won't take NO for an answer. These salesmen don't call in sick and they work all night without a break. No Social Security or sexual harassment lawsuits either. That's right, I was called by a computer!

The phrase, "Let's do lunch," has now been replaced with, "Have your computer call my computer." With voice mail and e- mail your computers can chat and you don't even have to come in contact with another living soul. Of course, over time this will destroy our social skills. Someone will simply say, *hello* and we'll all look around to see where the funny noise came from.

All this is why talk radio is so popular. People just want to have someone to talk to. Now days if you are lonely and want to express how you feel you dial a 900 number. Pay only $1.50 a minute and chat away to your heart's content. Be careful to enunciate each syllable however, so the computer on the other end of the line can understand you.

CASHING IN
THE CHIPS

I WAS FEELING a bit guilty about not attending church as often as I should, so I decided to do something religious for a change ... like play bingo!

What actually happened was that a local youth church group asked me to provide a cow for their annual fund raiser, Cow Plop Bingo, also known as Cow Flop Bingo. Admittedly, it was a "flop" but it was not my fault.

Americans will bet on anything, it seems, and the newest way to transfer wealth legally consists of turning a cow loose on a field of one hundred numbered squares. In this case, the squares had been sold to an unsuspecting public for one hundred dollars apiece. Obviously this is for people who have everything (but not for long). Whatever square the cow plops or flops in or on, the person who holds a ticket corresponding to the flopped upon number is the winner. And the winnings aren't chicken feed!

Churches and charities are not only condoning this newest form of gambling but are actually sponsoring the events, and it's easy to see why. They are excellent fund raisers. The winner gets to keep half the pot, in this case, $5,000, (minus taxes, of course) and the charity gets to keep the other half.

I was honored to have been asked to supply the cow who would select the winning number, so to speak. Cow Plop Bingo is the ideal game because it is high tech, entirely legal and difficult to rig. Trust me, I tried.

I believe that gambling is a sin only if you lose and because I had purchased a $100 ticket I tried to think of every way possible to insure that MY cow would "plop" on MY square. I selected my smartest cow for the event, Paint, so named because of her beautiful multi-colored hide. I worked with Paint diligently to teach her to read numbers and to move like a sheep dog with hand signals. But alas, my efforts were in vain.

Proper diet for the Bingo Cow is very important. The Bingo Cow must be fed just the right mixture of a laxative feed such as alfalfa and a binder such as oat hay because timing is everything in Cow Plop Bingo. The attention span of a group of gamblers is somewhere between three minutes and two hours and if they have to wait much longer waiting for a cow to plop the game loses some of its allure.

When the day of the big bingo game arrived I loaded up Paint in the trailer to take her to the Cowboy Casino which was an empty lot south of the church. The pastor explained the rules to the crowd and then passed the hat for the 100 participants to draw a number. The playing field was marked off with each square corresponding to a

Cashing In The Chips

player's number. The pastor also explained that he would be the judge in case of a "liner." A liner, he explained, occurs when the cow fails to plop within the well demarcated lines.

Bingo players lined the field as I prepared to turn Paint loose. The tension reached fever pitch and the minute Paint jumped out of the trailer and onto the playing field the crowd became unruly. "Over here," they yelled. "Number 14 please!" "Do it for me," read a sign. "No, not there," yelled the pastor.

Paint was confused, scared and surrounded on all four sides by a bunch of strangers yelling at her to make them rich by performing a normal body function. Paint was not used to this treatment and after she took one look at the shrieking throng she reacted as any normal cow would. She took off like a shot leaving her bingo markers deposited on 37 different squares.

I met her back at the ranch later but Paint hasn't been the same since that bingo game. She won't hardly eat, drink or plop. And when she does she expects to be paid for it. She's at home resting now, another tragic victim of the gambling game.

FIRST, LAST
AND ALWAYS

WHAT'S YOUR NAME?

It's probably your single most important possession yet you had absolutely nothing to do with its acquisition. You add or subtract from it with everything you do.

Names are handed down like cherished family heirlooms from one generation to the next. Immigrant families to this country often took their name from their first job in America. Today's Mrs. Carpenter may have had a long lost relative who once made his living sawing and hammering. A computer programmer named Smith may have descended from a long line of village blacksmiths.

Many immigrants shortened their birth names because they were too long, or because there was prejudice in their new country and they didn't want to be identified with a certain culture. Thus, Rothensteinkeiler became Roth. It would have been too long for a personalized license plate anyway. Others merely dropped or added a letter along the way. Descendants of John Wesley Hardin became

Harding, proving it is better to be named after a bad President than a first rate outlaw.

We refer to our monikers as "proper names" because that's how we should behave when representing our name … properly. I have always felt that you get better service from someone wearing a name badge because their performance is a reflection on their good name. I would much rather take my car to get worked on to a place named Smith's Automotive than one called One Minute Mechanics. You get higher quality when someone is proud enough to back their work with their name.

Many of the successful Fortune 500 companies still use a family name even though they aren't run by family members. What's a name like Campbell, Hilton or Ford worth, I wonder? The same can be said for newspapers and truck drivers. The best stories carry an author's byline. If a writer is proud of what he has written he wants his name on it. And have you noticed driving on life's highway that the most courteous truck drivers are the ones with their names and home towns painted on their doors? If the truck just displays the name of some conglomerate it becomes necessary for the company to put a bumper sticker on the back of the truck asking you to tattle if the driver isn't driving in a courteous fashion.

I don't trust people who change their names. Crooks and movie stars often do this. Crooks use aliases and movie stars use a stage name. It is no surprise to me that thespians change their names after seeing some of the junk coming out of Hollywood. If I posed nude in a movie, or acted in one that you would be ashamed to view while sitting with your family, I wouldn't want my real name on it either.

Hyphenated names are the latest fad. I can understand why a woman with a good name would be reluctant to give it up. I can't blame her for wanting to keep her own name, considering what some husbands have done to discredit theirs.

Think about your name the next time you ink your signature. A name is the first thing you are given and the only thing that really lives after you. It's on your birth certificate and your tombstone. It represents everything you achieved and it's what you will be remembered by. A fitting goal is to live such an exemplary life that future generations will want to name a child after you. What could possibly be a higher honor than to have your name followed by a Roman numeral? Or your first and last in combination with a surname not even related to your own, like George Washington Carver.

First, last and always a good name is to be cherished, protected and enhanced for future generations.

ABOUT THE AUTHOR...

LEE PITTS IS THE executive editor for Livestock Market Digest, a newspaper serving the livestock industry. He is the author of six previous books and a syndicated weekly humor column. His is a recognized byline in rural weekly newspapers and monthly magazines throughout the country. When not traveling down dirt roads in search of stories he makes his home in Los Osos, California, with his wife, Diane.

ABOUT THE ARTIST...

VEL MILLER IS AN award winning artist who draws inspiration from her fat burro, cow dogs, Quarter Horses and Longhorns. Her work reflects her authentic western lifestyle and everyday ranching experiences. Vel and her husband, Warren, own a coastal California ranch where they live the life celebrated in her art.